Slay Your Darlings:
An Anthology by the No Name Poets

Parson's Porch Books

Slay Your Darlings: An Anthology by the No Name Poets
ISBN: Softcover 978-1727610376
Copyright © 2016 by Sally Naylor, et.al.

All rights reserved. No part of this book may be reproduced or transmitted in any form or by any means, electronic or mechanical, including photocopying, recording, or by any information storage and retrieval system, without permission in writing from the publisher.

Cover Credits:
    Cover art by Cara Nusinov.

To order additional copies of this book, contact:

Parson's Porch Books
1-423-475-7308
www.parsonsporch.com

Parson's Porch Books is an imprint of Parson's Porch & Company (PP&C) in Cleveland, Tennessee. PP&C is an innovative company which raises money by publishing books of noted authors, representing all genres. All donations from contributors and profits from publishing are shared with the poor.

Slay Your Darlings:
An Anthology by the No Name Poets

ACKNOWLEDGEMENTS

Barbra Nightingale: Some Girl Named Natasha, *Poetrybay*; Song of the Mattress, *Poetry Bay*; My Daughter Calls Me Hag, *Rattle*; F, *Red Booth Review*.

Cara Nusinov: Maybe God, *Willow Review*.

Deborah DeNicola: John Baptizing Jesus, *Original Human* (Wordtech Press); Noli Me Tangere, *Original Human* (Wordtech Press); The Fallen Angel, *Where Divinity Begins* (Alice James Books); Final Longitude, *Original Human* (Wordtech Press).

Lenny DellaRocca: Dear Reader, *Dime Show Review*.

Gary Kay: Cassandra, *Litchfield Review*; Our Mother's Walk, *Write Room*.

Lori Schainuck: The Man-Seal, *Cold Mountain Review*.

Meryl Stratford: How Knowledge Enters the World, *The Magician's Daughter* (YellowJacket Press); Elegy with Backward Clocks, *Blue Hole*; Goldengrove, *The Magician's Daughter* (YellowJacket Press); Against Envy, *The Society of Classical Poets*; Her Education, *MALALA: Poems for Malala Yousafzei* (FutureCycle Press).

Sally Naylor: Largo, *Key West: A Collection*; Sugar, Salt, Life, *Rogue Nirvana* (Lioncrest Press); Summer of the Seventeen-Year Locusts, *Peregrine*; Elegy for Jim Hatch, *Dry Creek Review*.

Stephen Schaurer: O Urinal, *Author's Voice, WLRN radio & television*; NPR Creole, *Florida State Poetry Association Anthology # 32, WLRN radio & television*.

TABLE OF CONTENTS

Introduction	11

Barbra Nightingale

Some Girl Named Natasha	13
Song of the Mattress	14
My Daughter Calls Me Hag	15
Trip to the Toy Store	16
F	17

Cara Nusinov

Why Not Read a Poem for Breakfast?	21
Susurration	22
Maybe God	23
Raven	24
Poet Damaged	25

Deborah DeNicola

John Baptizing Jesus	29
Noli Me Tangere	30
The Fallen Angel	32
Final Longitude	34
The 23rd Psalm	36

Gary Kay

Cassandra	39
John Berryman Takes His Life	40
Our Mother's Walk	41
Galileo	42
Go Tell It	43

Lenny DellaRocca

Cynthia Cahn	47
Dear Reader	48
A Boy is a Fish	50
Garden and Storm	51
Night Sweats	52

Linda Baldwin Avila

Division	55
Dressing	56
Education in Mourning	58
World Opera House	59
Man in Red	60

Lori Schainuck
The Man-Seal   63

Marjorie Bloom
Cenotaph   67
Leo: Swan   68
Chicago Crosswalk   69
Infants of Ecuador in Miami   71
My Golden Palomino   73

Meryl Stratford
How Knowledge Enters the World   77
Elegy with Backward Clocks   78
Goldengrove   79
Against Envy   80
Her Education   81

Paul Saluk
A Date with My Poem   85
Resignation Letter   86
Existential Angst   87
Time   88
After This Poem Took Its First Breath   89

Sally Naylor
Largo   93
Mud Pies   94
Sugar, Salt, Life   95
Summer of the Seventeen-Year Locusts   96
Elegy for Jim Hatch   97

Stephen Schaurer
O, Urinal   101
A Most Fortunate Recipe for Zucchini Soup   102
Pot Roast Miami Blues   103
Pick This Poem Up Off the Floor   104
NPR Creole   106

Conclusion: Workshop Critique   109
Contributors   111

Slay your darlings.

--William Faulkner on revision

AN INTRODUCTION

Two girls, see, Deborah and Cara, too far
apart to meld words, so their poem lips are
bifurcated, which in poetry is
enjambment, clamor for a new critique group,
from a tri-county of poets, grab Lori and Paul
from another cluster, Meryl and Linda from
the worded winds of teaching and editing,
Gary the Prof (Barbra's too busy), Stephen who is
someone's relative, eight to start, who would seldom
be unanimous about anything, except smiles
of respect for words that dance, measures of rhythms,
inner lives exposed in hieroglyphs of poem.
Even their name, No Names, was voted upon (4-4 and a coin toss)
when no other title would do, nothing god forbid geographic,
nor similar to anything else, nor words already
spoken. So we called ourselves No Names and until this anthology
haven't used the title since. For what? We are
who we are. Plus additions, Lenny a page of Florida
poetry history, Sally and Margie who we discovered
in poetry workshops, Barbra the prof
who finally retired and has time. We meet. We
critique. If four of us agree that a line
should be deleted, at least one of us will feel
those words are the most important line in the poem.
A blithe balance. Then we go to dinner. To a
nameless place at least two of us don't like.
To the reader go our roils. Enjoy.

     Sept 12, 2009 plus seven orbits around the sun…

Barbra Nightingale

SOME GIRL NAMED NATASHA

You hear the name and right away
You feel snow and fur caps
Pulled over long, dark hair,
A foreign accent and lonesome
Miles of tundra, barren and cold.
You listen to the story and your breath
Comes out white clouds of frost.
You can't imagine the innocence,
The heartbreak in being naive,
And you want desperately
A happy ending, a Bullwinkle
Come to the rescue, but not this,
This boy standing before you,
This one so earnestly preaching
The virtues of giving to friends
In need, answering the call
With the last of his summer money.
You know then and there he's just a boy
With a moose of a heart, and secretly,
Oh so secretly, you're glad he is what he is.
Not a Boris in sight.

SONG OF THE MATTRESS

After the backaches and sprung
springs, after the tossing and turning,
the hours on the computer, searching,
the days rolling on different beds
which are really all the same beds
with different names in different stores,
after the comparing and the checking
one against the other, the merits
of this one versus that one, the price
points worth the difference (or not),
after the schmoozing and the angst
with the sales staff, the fear I've made
a bad deal, will regret it in a month
maybe two, I finally bought a bed.
Too bad I wasn't this careful with the mate.

MY DAUGHTER CALLS ME HAG

then the B-word, followed
by the C-word just before—
or is it after
I boiled her in oil, stewed
her up in a bowl served to her father?
That's one version.
Another says it's smoke and mirrors,
a classic pull-the-wool-
and-be-done-with-it story
straight from no one's mouth
tasting of nothing like truth.
But so it goes: her version,
my version,
the version before the sky fell,
the one before that, and at least
two or three that happened after.
I sit at my loom, counting stitches.
When I run out of numbers
perhaps I'll understand
how we came to this:
bone in our teeth,
gums dripping blood.

TRIP TO THE TOY STORE

And what a trip it was.
Just when you think
you've seen it all
there's anal bleach
G-spot massagers
sharp toothed nipple clips
with long tassels of chain
an obsessive three appendage plug,
nuggets, balls, rods of glass,
aluminum, or lifelike silicone
that flex and hum in five different speeds.
Who knew? Apparently I'm behind all the balls,
not just the eight.

F

Failure. Fornication. Faith.
There's a threesome! Effing
mouthful of euphemisms.
Mirror, mirror on the wall,
Who's the fairest of them all?
Effing bloody right, you are.
A fairy tale complete
with fanfare and farce,
drama and flourish, as if the fairies
gathered to dance in the dust—
a fictitious five-alarm fire
kicked up by their sparks.
Incandescent, fibrilant.
Fundamental as fractured rain.

Cara Nusinov

WHY NOT READ A POEM FOR BREAKFAST?

Why not read a poem for breakfast along with your oatmeal
and your bacon and eggs? After perusing The New York Times
satisfy your intellect on whimsical rhyme.
Politics with poem—we serve up the best, orange juice
and sports verse, dress and undress—

poets sculpt as the muse, any subject that is in the news . . .

SUSURRATION

Just typing s and u and then s and u,
then r, r, a,
calmed me down,
and I needed calming after
I realized that the whispering
was caustic and carried my name
as it floated to my ears on the breeze.

The resentment boiled,
made me hot under my mane.
I fluffed my hair up and down to cool off
like a flapper dancing in a speakeasy,
it fanned me, good.

How dare they screw up my life
when I just ironed out all the wrinkles
and was enjoying caressing the smooth
days and rustling velvet nights.

MAYBE GOD

is a

menopausal woman

with a beard

and lightning

is her hot

flashes, rain

her tears

and

she ignores

those she loves the most

since she's so frigging busy

with all the

    others

RAVEN

My favorite scarf
was knit of delicate Cashmere
woven rich as if for privileged princesses
and kings, wispy as a feather floating
on tides. It was as warm as a hug.

I wrapped my soul in its folds
and one day in the wind
of the Velvet Valley, a greedy gust,
stole the scarf like a Corvus
with prey in its beak and carried it
far above the trees.

Black like a Raven, my scarf wafted
and twirled away,
    away,
and like love lost in youth,

        it was gone.

POET DAMAGED

Sometimes she only half listens now, remembering has become so burdensome.
Like snowflakes melted on the windowpane, thoughts leave her

never

to be   thought

again.

As in opening a stubborn new jar, her memories stick, jammed in the turn, closed and slow. Trying to remember is of no use.
She jots down these words
    before
        they . . .

Deborah DeNicola

JOHN BAPTIZING JESUS

He must have been a sight,
> barbaric hair, dilated eyes (prelude
>> to Herodias' still life on the platter)

They say he lived on wild honey and the long torsos
> of locusts, that he dressed in fetid camel pelts
>> and rags and that he ranted

as if he had a finger in a messianic
> socket, his arm, a limb of lightning
>> in the shallows of the Jordan.

Then one day Jesus in his yellow hair. The whole head
> thundering under water, and heaven downloaded
>> between the bodies of two cousins,

baptist and carpenter,
> genetic tripwires sizzling, the Holy Spirit
>> furring vision, and then the Lord's voice

great blue whale
> breached on the banks of being. Rose light
>> on the mountains, all mythic harvest, sheen

and mystery, all potential in the instantaneous
> skating of the clouds, then recognition
>> as the boys, wet and electric,

nod to one another the unremitting readiness, the Now—
> and the ecstatic knowing.
>> The tragic ecstatic knowing.

NOLI ME TANGERE
The Gospel of John 20:14

There was a presence before the stone.
A pressure so much larger than human
wounds. My mind let go into the crags
of sorrow and I grew
this cavernous heart. It was a tomb
but also a garden.
One is the other
always. The spirit rises. The body stays
and blooms. I took him
for the gardener as the roses were wilted
on the lattice near where he stood.
He'd been broken and nailed
but nothing showed. Not one thorn,
not one bruise. The light stunned,
and magnetized me reaching for his robe.
He threw out his arm, a bolt
of lit wires—shocked—I fell back.
I wanted the warmth of his skin
to rest my head there,
but how removed he was, glowing
from his brow, both palms. No seams
for the ravaged flesh. The shade of white
on his garment, almost golden
like the air behind his head
where he taught us Truth.

No one dies. *No one*
ever dies. No one
is alone.

The painters only saw my body
as pulp, pigment and bone, the thick
color of my hair. But I was traveling
without movement, statue-still,
hardly there
while all my being
hummed. He said my name
and my head knocked
the sky. His gaze limbered my knees
and the suns in his eyes burned
through mine. I came to
myself alone, stupefied, not knowing when
he'd gone. And I ran to tell the brothers
we must choose belief, despite
the fears which fool our sense,
the fear which covered Eden up.

THE FALLEN ANGEL

after the photograph by Duane Michaels

She's leaning up in the island of her bed,
knees flung open through her French cut teddy
as if she had expected his arrival

through the huge room's starry window
where the radiator glows,
awakened, like her throat

with the sudden host of his tongue in her mouth.
Naked, he's climbed astride her, pulpy wings
strapped to his back and belted round his belly—

If that's a drawback, well,
that's how he got here, winged it—
through a down draft in the alley

and you take what you get sometimes.
She's up for it anyways, up on her elbows,
her many fingers, gasping fish, replenished

by new waters, *and God, I'd take him*
whoever he is—Zeus, Apollo, Hermes—
gold ringletted hair, maple tree of a torso,
left hand, a wand, casting a spell across her nipple—
But what do I know from sex? It's been a while.

Are angels safe?
Can that plaid woolen blanket maintain
room temperature beneath their weight?
Or will it steam and hydroplane like a magic carpet

launching—Watch those falling pillows
tilt the floor
as if some prime mover

ordained a radiant resurrection,
sun coming up, white-out backdrop,
already the eight foot windows burning.

Her soul is sold,
though dressed in down-home wings, she thinks
he may be an imposter—Still,

Manhattan slumbers there
suspended like heaven
and his webbed fingers probe

the dimple in her chin,
propping her sweet face eternally under his
so this moment might never end
though if it does—
she'll have this sky-scraping simian
in the loft of her memory. This horny dream,

this shifty apparition, luciferous
spectre in diaphanous flesh—and yes
God yes, I'm jealous.

FINAL LONGITUDE

There are broken rosaries in my dreams.
We are up to our knees in murky water and the rain
has been poisoned, sallowing our skin with pesticides.
All your life you've been immunized from risk, waiting
for the roof to fall. Listen, it's possible the past will always
carry its cross uphill and the future is just a phantom in an evening dress
seen through stained glass. No doorbell, no mail slot will let her in.

The truth is you have only these small moments fallen in your lap,
swarms of fireflies you've brushed aside without notice.
It is time now to take the measure of their wings. Time to realize
we are blessed with an aria only the two of us can sing. I want us to laugh
and call out each other's names in the wind that never stops
messing up our hair, our clothes. Let's remember flesh

coming together, what it is that humans do mixing their limbs,
how a man dips into a woman in a room lit by touch, and sunlight
shifts through curtains where the pattern is latticed
so even the shadows on the ceiling climb out of their bodies,
above gravity and time. Can't you feel the fear again tonight

on the evening news warning us not to trust the streets.
Not to reach for the healing lotion of another's arms
without some notarized adherence to the rules. Fine print
is full of bars in the jails we are taught to believe in.
I am weary of elusive words and wary
of a world that doesn't want my miracles.

There is a border to the territory
of you, a final longitude
and I am headed there.

THE 23RD PSALM

One night we memorized the 23rd psalm,
reciting in unison over and over. Stumbling often
while watching each other's eyes. You bought
that tiny book in the crowded store in Ogunquit
that 4th of July. Beatrice Potter's drawings,
little rabbits in green pastures shall-not-wanting
and tables with set places to dine among rivals.
We whispered in bed in your dark apartment,
laughing at lines we forgot, *he encourageth my soul* . . .
thy rod and thy staff . . . *my cup runneth under*
. . . *the days of our lives* . . .
You later gave it to your dying father. Or rather,
your sweet, lying-down-all-day-senile
father. And how he adored it! The bunnies
in fluffy skirts and short red pants, smiling figures
with straw hats waving bouquets of carrots, lakes
as green as Kinnereth off the shores of Capernum,
far from Gethsemene, Calvary, The Dome of the Rock.
Just small Potter people suggesting—
as in Christ's recommending to grown ups
how much like little children we could become.

Gary Kay

CASSANDRA

Inside the gates pale women speak
of heroes.
Of me they whisper
bitch,
robed in doom.

What choice had I?
I gave these Trojans what was bred in me.

When the city's filled with flames,
my blood will lie
on the damp queen's marble floor.
The earth, my spinning wheel,
will rest.
The stars above my head
will still refuse to bend.

JOHN BERRYMAN TAKES HIS LIFE

University of Minnesota.
Arts Theater Lecture: Monday 7 P.M.
Topic: The Art of Metaphor in Poetry
Speaker: John Berryman

Berryman steps up to the podium.
No notes in his hands.
"*You're a rat* is an example
of a metaphor," he says.
Then walks away

Soon came darker days—
unopened bottles of booze
crying out beneath the bed.
Mountains across a river
saying:
It takes only a few minutes
to be man.

On the day of his death,
a note to his wife:

Dear Kate, you did all you could.
I'm unemployable, a nuisance.
Be well, be happy, remarry.
Minneapolis bridge that night.
John Berryman standing tall.
Sober as a rat.

OUR MOTHER'S WALK

One night our mother
must have fallen in love
with a stranger.
She left after supper.
Came back when the sun
rose high in the east.

She stood in the wide open doorway.
Her hair was wild and pink.
One hand squeezed the doorknob,
the loose one waved goodbye
to someone we never did see.

GALILEO

I say to the men in clean dark robes, muttering
scriptures as they pace, and to that idiot the Pope:
    The sun's the center of the universe.

My mind was once a burning torch.
This telescope lit the flames.
Now my eyes give way to darkness,
and blazing crosses
do battle with night.

But I can still recall
Lord, the miracles
I've seen—
The cratered moon with ice-floes in its veins.
Four moons of Jupiter.
The sun with infinite
dark spots
ravaging its face.

GO TELL IT

to the Pope, the Bishops
and the nuns. Tell it to Mohammed,
Maimonides, Luther,
Karl Marx.

Scream it to Hitler and Stalin.
Whisper it to the Russian farmers,
and the Jews.

Debate it with Camus
and Jean Paul Sartre.
Point a finger at Derrida.

Text Obama, Taylor Swift,
Bill Gates, Mark
Zuckerman.

Then go to the river.
Sit down.
Don't breathe
a syllable.

See what the river does.

Lenny DellaRocca

CYNTHIA CAHN

She gazed like some gypsy-actress.
Cherub-like she almost hovered
while gilded images
haunted her apocalyptic lines.

She whispered—
the square root of my death—
and—
This is where queens come to drown—
spoons froze mid-cup,
not a door ached shut.

An immaculate presence
lingered like a summer
afternoon of sex and jazz.

I was there that day
and applauded long and loud
the last of her.

DEAR READER

I wanted to dazzle you
with saints and witches
impress you with Mayan
priests carving into the teeth
of young girls to inlay
chips of blue jade.

I gave you a man who
carried a ladder
all over the world
propping it against cathedrals
to climb to the moon,
submerging it into the sea
to the other side of the world.

My fear of heights
could've been a poem
but I gave you some
apocryphal joker
in a tree with a broom.

I'm the Oliver Hardy
of poetry squashed by
the piano of nonsense
at the bottom of literary stairs.

I feel like a man who sees
a picture of his wife
in the newspaper, dark
sunglasses, blonde wig, handcuffs,
married to a spy in Europe.

I apologize. I should have known
all the fancy lines in the world

can't make a bad poem
more than the sum of its words.

A BOY IS A FISH

He chooses among
a pantheon of lures

until a certain hook
feels like home
in his mouth

the way a woman's name
shimmers in a man's voice

the boy's lips will bleed.

Many lines and nets
will pull him out of water—

girls, books, poems, gods—
each an airless place
each a kind of wound.

GARDEN AND STORM

Daffodil-lightning,
earth and weather,

your mouth is a river
of air and words

streaming through my heart.
I grow in your voice

dandelion strong.
The river heals

all windy days.
Say something love,

or only hum
and I'll sleep to wake

in the lush moment
of your kiss.

NIGHT SWEATS

Dec 18, 1996

> They wake me up again—the people upstairs—2:15 a.m.—from a dream I can't remember now because of the noise they make. The bed's rusted springs. The insidious screeching. He is torturing her. Crucifying her with his cock. Pinning her to that goddamned bed. Pinning. She needs to be fucked.

Dec. 21, 1996

> Again. And I have already gone upstairs to complain. The other night. 4 a.m. when I pounded my fist against the jalousie glass in his door. Pounded. I awoke the father, but it was the son I wanted to kill. And the handsome boy in his expensive blue robe came to the cool night air. You are murdering my sleep, I said. With loud birds. With a mad red army. His hair not even messed, black as nails in the dark, black as night frantic with a woman who cannot be controlled, who must be impaled.

Dec. 28, 1996

> It is the sound of agony when something used up is forced to work, a machine's un-oiled parts smoked dead, locked up, pushed beyond that which it was made to do. Brakes grinding past the light down a dark road where the car smashes. Not even the voices of the driver and his anorexic girl can be heard. Only the car. Only the bed. Only Jesus nailed to the cross at ungodly hours.

Linda Baldwin Avila

DIVISION

You take the steak knives, I'll take the forks and spoons.
While you slash at me with knives, I'll stick you
with forks and spoon out your guts to feed the children.

Take the quilt, I keep the sheets and towels. You need
the quilt to warm your cold heart, while I'll use the sheets
to clean off the slime you throw at me.

I'll swim in the ocean and you can keep the pool
with its chlorinated water. Maybe the chlorine will
clean your soul while the ocean sets me free to rock
on the waves and learn to surf.

DRESSING

I loved playing "dress-up" when I was little, putting on a dress
my mother wore as a bridesmaid, or the frilly garments and suede
heels that came in a trunk my mother bought at an estate sale.

The movie-star paper dolls I played with came wearing printed
bathing suits. Betty Grable's was red. The red didn't show through
the sturdy paper of the filmy blue gown, or the white

day dress that was held in place with fold-down tabs.
When I first started shopping for myself I didn't understand
clothing sizes or my body. I bought a skirt and rolled

the waist down. Cinched it with a belt to hold it up and make it short
enough. The turquoise knit skirt and top fit me so well that the looks
I got from older boys made me feel awkward.

I began to buy for the life I lived but desire for the life
I wished I lived sometimes triumphed in the dressing room.
Suits and dresses wore out and were replaced, while evening

gowns hung in the back of the closet with price tags attached.
In the times I lived alone in an apartment, I often didn't dress,
cleaning, reading, cooking in the nude. Windows weren't

a problem, they faced brick walls or were curtained. I've moved beyond
classic and dressy clothing, don't live that way anymore. I like

jeans and t-shirts and my windows open to the sun.
I'm re-thinking how I want to appear in public and spend time
staying in touch with my energy body—balancing and keeping
it healthy and elastic—and now feel fully clothed, imprinted

with the skin stretched over my bones.

EDUCATION IN MOURNING

The Sugar Maple withered and died.
The Norway Spruce was torn
from the ground by tornado winds.
Flowers do not last, the grass browns,
the earth buries and snow covers over.

WORLD OPERA HOUSE

It's been open forever presenting dramas for all ages—classical plays, opera, ballet, musicals, comedy, farce, circuses, even wrestling, street dance, soap operas. You want to see the show, that's where you go. Some patrons began to push actors into parts they wouldn't normally play, didn't want to play or weren't suited for, or removed a pivotal actor, installing another in the part. No one stood up to the patrons. This behavior morphed into petty pilfering, like slipping a spoon from the coffee bar into your pocket. Soon even some cast members started looting the theater. Gilded moldings, chandeliers, seats, props, and scenery disappeared. Rather than let shows go on with what was left, production crews took to renting scenery and props back from those who'd done the looting. The patrons were happy to profit, ever ready to raise rental rates. When patrons, casts and crews realized ransoms could buy what used to be free, nothing was safe. Greed can't imagine the future. Looters are even now removing the floor, and the roof. The walls are ghostly. This theater will soon be no more, the cast, the crews, even the patrons falling into nothingness.

MAN IN RED

Dad loved red, especially red
shirts. If he didn't wear a red
flannel shirt, he'd put on a red
cap, or wear a red bandana.

He didn't wear red pants,
but what he wore worked.
He was a ladies man, and never
had trouble attracting women.

"Women attracted to men in red, research shows . . .
Women view men in red as higher in status,
more likely to make money, more likely to climb
the social ladder. This is true across the globe,
even for other primates."*

He made money enough,
but had no interest
in society. He cried poor,
drove old cars and trucks.

But, he did know how to troll for women.

*"What could be as alluring as a lady in red? A gentleman in red," finds a multicultural study published Aug. 2, 2011 in the *Journal of Experimental Psychology*.

Lori Schainuck

THE MAN-SEAL

A crescent-shaped thing sat in a tree. The man asked, is it a flying saucer?
In the crisscross of a high branch: a bird's nest.
It resembled honey strings the bees might have whipped up.
Or burnt pastry. And what would that be doing in a tree?
      The man held a forlorn eggshell—
      the thing pulsed between his fingers.

He surmised a thing is only what we assign it, our transcendence
only a moonbeam, counter-wise
he concluded he was a seal. His body shape shifted. Flesh melted.
He touched his hair. Only whiskers. Feet: flippers. Skin: a waxy
blubber. Day stormed into dusk. The sky: a big eggplant.
      Seals don't eat
      eggplant, he thought. Then: thunder, thunder—poof!

The green-leafed trees now coated in whiteness. The houses vanished.
Cars lifted. Attached themselves to the mighty magnet-clouds.
He leaped into the full void of moisture
      as if he dived into a melted ice cube.
      Ice sheets, a glacier of blueness—

a man inside a seal's body in a Nordic country.
Other seals welcomed him. He mated, made man-and-woman seals,
in winter he ate fish, in springtime wildflowers and berries.
One day he longed for his wife's homemade coleslaw,
      his newborn's little piano-key toes—
      whistle of jays in the old oaks.

The man-seal (still vested with reason) thought animals were lower beasts.
He glanced into the bounded oblivion. Can a seal talk to God?
The night sky is a shadow box, he reckoned. He tapped on its hinge.
    It opened, a fireball beamed. Like a supernova
        he whirled back into the quiet wilderness of his former life.

Marjorie Bloom

CENOTAPH

Mother, my eyes close and your brown eyes come to me,
lit & then unlit, lid-shaded & lusterless, but you still stand
tall as a far-off cenotaph, in your Warrior Pose.

Your once quick mind repeats itself, or circumlocutes, not
you, it repeats itself. Glass splinters of your old self, until
you're distant, unreachable, finally, untouchable too.

Mother, I name you *Warrior of Mind's Long Night*,
as if you embody a yoga pose, one that demands
you engage each synapse, & at times, you must torc to hold.

LEO:SWAN

word photo after Annie Leibovitz' Leonardo and the Swan

Leo's intense eyes, shadows underneath. His furrowed brow. Look at his hair... as if someone's fingers went through and pulled it back from a widow's peak, then combed it back and over to the right. And the firmset jaw, fine-angled all the way up to cheekbones. Now touch his sensuous tight mouth. I look at him as hard as he looks at me. He wears a black turtleneck. A white swan drapes across his body. Like a necklace, amulet, shocking charm, the s-shaped neck curves, surrounds Leo's neck. The swan's eye is open, but looks down. The swan face near the boyish face. The bird's big body softly bends into the boyman body, white breast on chest, hands gently enfold. Leo holds the swan: the swan holds Leo. Leo calms the swan: the swan calms Leo. In the background some high, wild grasses appear, bend, then blur. Silent intense young man. Mute swan, out of water not in air. The two move forward, slight anterior thrust to exit the frame and enter our lives. How mysteriously, how fiercely, they tame.

CHICAGO CROSSWALK

An old lady appears
in the thick of the throng.
While deep in the surge
her legs in white hose
shuffle quick as they can
but slower by far
than counted seconds
of a traffic light.

She heels side-to-side
her own safe harbor
in her wide cotton skirt
pink & white striped
puffed out like a Sunfish
full-sail over water.

But the neon count is up.
I raise my palm
stop cars taxis buses
while her seaweed scarf
with those yellow dots
drags toward the curb.

Then slowly
she ascends
high stately steps.

Once inside The Art Institute

she glides up an escalator

way up to the ceiling

& there she prevails—

lighthouse beaming

across polished museum floors

INFANTS OF ECUADOR IN MIAMI

after Leonard Nathan

One day

through windows slashed

wide open

I heard

from your creches&cradles

Incan chants

feathery lulls

mesmers of hibiscus tongues

I heard

I heard

your zithers&humms

wave high in unison

over

oleander

I heard

your even tones

slope

down

Miami's

red-tiled

roofs.

The next day

alone on the street

I peered

into all the city strollers.
Were you the girl
whose mouth made an O?
Or the boy
who blubbered his lips?
I searched
I searched
for small *cantadores*.

Out of silence
your music still quivers
your *a cappella* rises&rounds
rounds&rises
as my empty arms lift to hold—
only opal air.

MY GOLDEN PALOMINO
MY RED PASHMINA SHAWL

I wish I had my palomino
I have my red pashmina shawl

my palomino took me away
my pashmina keeps me warm

palomino's coat was golden
with paler mane and tail

pashmina's red as hibiscus
in high summer bloom

I see my golden palomino
high hard rider on his back

hard rider goads my palomino
his whip's oddly razor quick

he rides my horse so hard
so hard my palomino falls

fold my red pashmina shawl
over my golden palomino

cry for my red palomino
cry for my golden pashmina

I had my golden palomino
I have my red pashmina shawl

Meryl Stratford

HOW KNOWLEDGE ENTERS THE WORLD

Bobby, age seven. All boy:
toy cars and building blocks.
Too quiet today, up in his room
alone. He's sprawled on the floor,
a book open before him.
Snakes. He turns the page. Long
scaly bodies, limbless, lidless.
How they shed their skins,
swallow their prey whole,
flicking their forked tongues.
Ribbon Snakes. Garter Snakes.
A graceful Green Snake weaving
through branches and weeds. A Black Racer
holding its head high as it slithers
swiftly over the ground. An Indigo Snake
with a mouse in its jaws. Rattlesnakes,
how they coil before striking. Even a
dead rattler can bite.

At last a book that tells a boy
things he needs to know.

ELEGY WITH BACKWARD CLOCKS

The clocks have fallen back.
The white clock ticking on the kitchen wall,
the antique clock in the living room.
They've fallen back as leaves fall,
as darkness falls earlier each night.
The bedside alarm with its shrill voice
and luminous face, the pocket watch,
the cuckoo clock with raucous bird
and Bavarian dancers. After the fiction
of saving daylight, we've returned to facts.
Once we rose with the sun, marked time
by its shifting shadow. Now we have clocks.
Now we have months instead of moons.
We've abandoned the fantasy that we
could save some of the daylight,
even an hour of it. That we could live
our evenings in the light of the past,
borrow light from the past to postpone
for awhile the coming of darkness.
These autumn days would last forever
if we called them by another name.

GOLDENGROVE

And yet you will weep and know why.

                         - Gerard Manley Hopkins

The lesson for today is *grief*.
I write the word, *i* before *e*,
on the board. One of the children's fathers
has died. I went to the funeral,
watched her follow the casket, crying
for him, enclosed in that heavy box,
carried away. Now her classmates
write about grief. They bow to the task
like young trees in a strong wind,
grip pencils that are mightier than swords.
Words march in solemn procession
along blue paths through white storms.
After the last sentence, they look up
as if they've come back from far away.
The room is quiet. No one fidgets
or laughs as they stand, one by one,
to read with quivering voices, through tears,
their stories of divorced parents, lost
dogs, and the grandmothers they loved.

AGAINST ENVY

Never envy the peacock. It cannot fly.
Beautiful bird, but the peacock cannot sing.
The song of the peacock is a loud harsh cry.

Pale birds, buoyant in morning's endless sky,
climb, soaring and drifting, wing on wing.
Never envy the peacock. It cannot fly.

Small birds open their beaks at dawn. They vie
with melodies that make the woodlands ring.
The song of the peacock is a loud harsh cry.

Wild birds ride on winds that carry them high
above the hills. They visit the Mountain King.
Never envy the peacock. It cannot fly.

Tame birds in jeweled cages greet the eye
of night with quiet notes that cluster as they cling.
The song of the peacock is a loud harsh cry.

The peacock complained to Juno. She told him why:
Beauty is yours. You can't have everything.
Never envy the peacock. It cannot fly.
The song of the peacock is a loud harsh cry.

HER EDUCATION

Into the quiet classroom
of the mind comes flying
the furious teacher with a lesson
of fear. This *bullet*
is not a bullet, it's merely
a word, something the mouth
makes for the delicate ear,
something the breath sends
that troubles the air, a ballet
of sound moving through silence
that explodes in an image as sudden
as death. Where is the wound?
It bleeds in the minds of a million
grief-stricken girls. They will be
pilots, doctors, warriors,
poets. They will sit on the ground
in the dust, just to learn.
In the twenty-first century,
every girl is Malala.

Paul Saluk

A DATE WITH MY POEM

Did you ever begin a poem excited
like a teen ready for a date with
the girl of his dreams?

Each word tingles.
Every line a promise of
the warmth of her skin.

Your pulse leaps as you finish the poem.
And like the promise of a second
date, you

re-read the poem

only to find that you were
stood up.

This is one of those poems.

RESIGNATION LETTER

I wrote a Letter of Resignation to a company I did not work for. They searched the HR Department files for my file. They searched the archives for my file. When they couldn't find it they had to create a new file. And, then they could call me in for an exit interview, which they did. And I dressed appropriately. Blue suit, red tie, polished black shoes. They asked why I was leaving. I told them that I felt overlooked. They expressed regret. Said that I was not a troublemaker. Wished me luck, and gave me two-weeks severance pay.

EXISTENTIAL ANGST

Here you are, once again
wide awake
in the fear of the night. You

toss and turn in the silence and in
the dark that seems to know
something that you do not.

You wonder the why and
what of who you are. And,

who you are not. Uncertain of
what matters and what does not.

But then, you
roll over and touch
the smooth, silky skin
of your lover.

Well, maybe
sometimes it doesn't matter
what doesn't matter.

TIME

I said to Time:

I see you everywhere.
When I go to sleep. When
I get up. When I

miss the bus but see
the next one and think,
"Am I too early or too late?"

I see you in my
greying. In my son's
son's tiny fingers.

Even in my mother's
old photographs.

But now Science says you
don't exist. What am I
not seeing?

Time replied:

Does it really matter?

AFTER THIS POEM TOOK ITS FIRST BREATH

I was able to smother it

before it cried,
before it lamented lost souls,
before its conceit of epiphany,
before it fell in love with itself,
before it told you the wisdom you already knew,
before it revealed the secrets of things unknowable,

but not before it got this far.

Sally Naylor

LARGO

You are entering a state of mind

reads the sign at mile marker three.
Latitude: twenty-four degrees.
New Year's Eve. Fisherman's Trail.
The man who lives with two women
in the stilt house next door knocks
over his beer, cusses out the blonde.
Down in the yard his big black Lab
chases her she-goat, saucer-eyed
with fear, into the chain link fence.
The goat stumbles, harried by the Lab,
its own bleatings, reedy rasps,
wheezings, and the blonde's dry sobs.
No more Bogies and no Bacall.
Neon billboard over the house reads:

Paradise regained: The Florida Keys.

MUD PIES

I advise a novice to revise,
as Faulkner said, to slay your darlings,
while embracing imperfection,

to practice the art of saying in words
what can't be said. To do it well,

first write on the head of an angel or pin. Right it write or upside down.
Invoke mud pie metaphor. Locate some surreal playground. Dig deep.
Smooth your sticky patties, sculpt and pat as mud splatters. Play.

Temper cravings for coronation in white space or by the academy,
divorce all errant longings for literary orgasm,
forget the Blake-Whitman transcendence traditions
or any other hyper-scrupulous, gold-plated ostentations.

Slay your darlings, embrace, then discard the flawed.

Grab any passing, unmarried muse, Bunny Hop, Two-Step, then Waltz,
Boogie, Hockey-Pokey, Hully Gully, or Twist again, get down, get wonky

                                                then tango right off that set.

SUGAR, SALT, LIFE

So I'm at Don Giovanni's waiting for my *insallata frutta del mare dulce*, sitting in full sun, and it's joyful to say it with my college Italian intact, so much more vibrant, less effete than the French, while preposterous dog twins—two sets—trot by, walking their owners. I've come from my Guardian Angel. Captured her image on my iPhone, the real deal hangs regally in bas relief from the façade of the Guardian Angel Church in Chelsea, I flew up to her, slipped into her skin, and continued my trek, within half a block I spy the art guy with a truckload of large canvases and sense how easy it would be to live here, how this energy is me, the big me, the beyond the bright body of me or the temple of me, the possibility of me, the feist, vibration, contribution and vamp of me. And I say yes to New York without a plan. I am grateful to your Sikh cab drivers in red turbans, to your Islamic women in their head gear wolfing down pastrami with their large bodies and families at Katz's. NYC: tolerant of your beliefs & judgmental of your shoes, declares a mini storage mural. I hear an Irish brogue and spot guys with dreads, a woman with nine-month baby belly sports Madonna heels. Oh Gotham, I am delirious—you don't mess around. Neither do I. Time to exit stage left. Hear our chorus now: heal or die.

SUMMER OF THE SEVENTEEN-YEAR LOCUSTS

Headed for the Maryland coast
round about midnight
we ran right into them.

Embracing the murmuring
world, our earth became a shroud
of thrumming husks,
turned soon enough
under the tires into a sort of oil.

Caught in our fine car
and bad marriage,
grateful for no traffic,
wild to be anywhere else,

we slid in a slow ricochet
across both lanes,
death by brittle death.

ELEGY FOR JIM HATCH

I was taxed by your ill-timed, bawdy innuendoes
in mock-falsetto whispers, by your obesity and bad teeth.
Tonight I leaf through your copy of *The Art of Eating*,
a dog-eared volume offered as compensation

for your vaunted caviar pie, the one you never
got around to making. I loved you anyway. This bookmark
half hides the chapter on "How to be Cheerful Though Starving."
It's the handmade label from a jar of sweet & sour tarragon mustard,
contents: eggs, sugar, mustard, vinegar,
dated 6/5/89, signed Jim. Red-headed, piquant
like your cooking, you were an anarchy that believed
in institution: this book, that label and a note
in your hand is all I have left. You wasted away
so quickly: died dirty and alone in Italy.

Not even Byron would have thought it romantic.
Yet I hear you wrangle still with your correct
Princetonian, Episcopal God, having cooked and kept your wolf
at bay for fifty years. Sleep well, old sweet and sour.

Stephen Schaurer

O, URINAL

O, O, O, Miami,
I should have used the men's room
before I left the restaurant
where we sipped cocktails in glasses
as big as lampshades,
and now, a few blocks up Ocean Drive
through a flow of torches and tables,
this is where I ask a drag queen
for the nearest restroom.
She tells me she's Geraldine,
Queen of South Beach,
as she takes my hand,
pulls me into the pulsating neon,
down a corridor
where she gentles me through a door—
a unisex powder room with a urinal,
thank god,
and I could just kiss her, but I don't.

A MOST FORTUNATE RECIPE FOR ZUCCHINI SOUP

I was invited to dinner to laugh
at his sick jokes, beside his bedeviled
wife and their friend the priest,
to make it a foursome.

Over nutmeg spiced zucchini soup
the priest told his tale about a troubled couple
he had prayed through their problems,
who invited him to supper, to meet the family,
four kids and a dog, but when he knocked
no one came or barked, so he called his way in,
finding blood-splattered walls, bodies in their beds.

I was fortunate to get her recipe for zucchini soup,
before she and the priest committed suicide . . .

Saute *1 cup chopped crying onion*
in *½ cup butter* until heartbroken.
Stir in *2 ½ cups liberated chicken stock*,
1 ½ pounds small zucchini, shredded, shredded, shredded.
Add gusto: *2 tsp basil, ½ tsp salt, ½ tsp nutmeg, ¼ tsp white pepper.*

Recite "A Happy Priest Does His Best Work in Hell" until boiling.
Puree in portions, leave lumpy like life.
Sinfully desirable hot or cold.
Serves a family of six.

POT ROAST MIAMI BLUES

I'm making pot roast
in a crockpot,
peppering chunks of chuck,
with new potatoes, pearl onions,
chopped celery and parsley,
Susan Waggoner's recipe,
the passionless prostitute
in *Miami Blues*,
who just lay on the bed,
her groin greased,
sherry in the gravy,
for you to do with her what you will,
her insatiable appetite not disrobed
until she sprinkled in her secret touch,
a tiny pinch of curry powder,
then she stirred.

Note: Chuck roast ingredients are from the novel *Miami Blues* by Charles Willeford, 1988, page 127, prepared by the prostitute Susan Waggoner.

PICK THIS POEM UP OFF THE FLOOR

No one speaks English in the Cuban bakery
where I order *veinticuatro pastalitas de guayaba*.
It is near closing and the displays are empty,
but the noisy lady I have never seen before
folds a box and takes it to the back counter.

From a rolling rack filled with trays of pastries
she fills my box with her dirty fingers,
drops a pastalita on the floor,
picks it up and tosses it back on the tray,
then fills the rest of the box
including the pastalita from the floor.

When she brings me the box I raise my arms and shout "No!"
She questions a baker who comes from the back.
I tell him what she did.
He rushes off to the ovens, calling to someone
as I leave in disgust.

The bakery is closed
when I wonder if the man understood,
when I wish I had videoed the counter clerk,
when I wish I had stayed to demand she be fired,
and the dirty pastalitas destroyed.
I call and leave a message; I send a long e-mail.

How many times have I walked out too early?
Before the impossible touchdown,
before they called my raffle number,
before my father passed away,
before the girl who loved me got off the train.

I need to carry a portable anchor
to all scenes of impending joy and disaster.

NPR CREOLE

That's so Miami,
the lull of French voices
on nighttime NPR,

the sound-poetry of their music,
like soft-breezed waves onto beaches.

I dream of the stories they tell.

And then I am told,
it is the Miami-Dade Public Schools,
speaking in Creole.

Still I pretend, I listen,
for the purrs of the poems I first imagined.

CONCLUSION: WORKSHOP CRITIQUE

You read your poem to the workshop. One by one they propose suggestions: runaway echoes in your head. *Is that "read" or "read"? Take out one of the "suggestions". No, I like that. Maybe there shouldn't be a line break here. Does that actually work? Maybe a question mark here. No, I think it is a statement. Okay then, but let the reader decide. I don't think that last sentence is necessary. Is that a question or a statement? There are too many "do"s. I don't see that. Come on, it's the voice! Sorry to say, this makes no sense. I disagree, it certainly does. Better yet. Omit the first two stanzas and the last line. The poem really ends after the last line.*

CONTRIBUTORS

Barbra Nightingale's poems have appeared in *Rattle, Kansas Quarterly, Lummox, Poetry Bay, Sliver of Stone, Red Booth Review, Many Mountains Moving, The Florida Review, Mississippi Review* and others. Her newest collection, *alphalexia*, is forthcoming from Finishing Line Press, in 2017. Previous books include *Geometry of Dreams* (Word Tech), and *Two Voices, One Past* (YellowJacket Press). She is a Professor Emeritus from Broward College.

Cara Nusinov, mom, grandma, writer, teacher, artist, presents poetry and art workshops. She's co-founder/MC of THE POETRY BU*ffET* PARTY, is a prize winning photographer, Certified Poetry Therapy Practitioner, laughter yoga leader, read her poetry on NPR during National Poetry Month and other venues. Cara helped facilitate a book fair, free-lanced as a reporter/poetry columnist for The Pinecrest Tribune, authored *Unrequited Loves and other French Kisses*, was chosen for the "Coconut Grove Peacock Tour 2010" creating a unique traveling collage/anthology/ sculpture, The Polka Dot Poetry Peacock, which further initiates her mission to introduce poetry to as many people as possible.

Deborah DeNicola is the author of 2 full collections of poetry, most recently, *Original Human,* 2010 from Word Tech, *Where Divinity Begins* from Alice James Books, four chapbooks, and her memoir, *The Future That Brought Her Here* (NicholasHays) 2009. She edited *Orpheus & Company; Contemporary Poems on Greek Mythology* (UPNE.) An adjunct professor, and editor, DeNicola received The Carpe Articulum Award in 2010, Briar Cliff Poetry Award, 2007, the Santa Barbara Poetry Award, 2008 and The Paul Hoover Critical Essay Award from Packingtown Review, 2009. She is the recipient of an artist's fellowship from the *NEA*. Web site is www.intuitivegateways.com

Gary Kay was born in Winnipeg, Manitoba and relocated to South Florida, where he earned a Masters in Reading and Doctorate in Reading at the Community College from Florida Atlantic University. He taught at Broward Community College for 30 years and was also an adjunct at Florida Atlantic University and Nova Southeastern University. At Broward he won two Endowed Teaching awards and was voted professor of the year. His poetry has been published in 27 journals.

Lenny DellaRocca has had poems in numerous literary magazines since 1980 including: *Poet Lore, Poetrybay, Albatross, 2River view, Fairy Tale Review, Chiron Review, Seattle Review, POEM, Laurel Review, Apalachee Review, Sun Dog, Gulf*

Stream Magazine, *Mad Hat*, *Wisconsin Review*, *Maryland Poetry Review*, *Long Island Quarterly*, *The Potomac* and *Nimrod*. He is a Pushcart Prize nominee and his chapbook, *The Sleep Talker*, is available at Night Ballet Press. His latest collection, *Blood and Gypsies* is available from Anaphora Literary Press. DellaRocca is founder and co-publisher of *South Florida Poetry Journal- SoFloPoJo* and *Interview With a Poet* both at southfloridapoetryjournal.com

Linda Baldwin Avila grew up in northwestern Pennsylvania and forged a career in New York City where she co-founded a successful publishing company, since sold. She now lives in South Florida. She's studied poetry at The New School for Social Research with Richard Tayson and Malena Morling and also at workshops with Sharon Olds, Kevin Young, and Thomas Lux. Her poems have been published in *The Clackamas Literary Review*, *The South Carolina Review*, *The Cape Rock*, *The California Quarterly*, on-line in *Eclectica*, and the *South Florida Poetry Journal*.

Lori Schainuck lives and writes in Miami, Florida. "The Man-Seal" first appeared in *Cold Mountain Review*, Fall 2015.

In addition to making poems, **Marjorie Bloom** loves to translate Apollinaire's calligrams. Her translation of one such calligram, "The Stabbed Dove and the Water Fountain", appeared online in *Mead: The Magazine of Literature and Libation*s (Spring, 2014). Marjorie is a Registered Nurse who lives in South Florida.

Meryl Stratford's chapbook, *The Magician's Daughter*, won the 2013 YellowJacket Press Contest for Florida Poets. Her poems have appeared in *Rattle*, *Amsterdam Quarterly*, *Earth's Daughters*, *The Comstock Review*, *Connecticut River Review*, *Snail Mail Review*, *The Enigmatist*, and *Poetrybay*, and have been anthologized in *Crossing Lines* (Main Street Rag), *MALALA: Poems for Malala Yousafzai* (FutureCycle Press), *Adrienne Rich: A Tribute Anthology* (Split Oak Press) and *Glass Bottom Sky* (YellowJacket Press) among others. Meryl lives with her husband, Richard Magesis, in Hallandale Beach, Florida. She is an associate editor for *SoFloPoJo*, southfloridapoetryjournal.com

Paul Saluk is a retired Scientist and Businessman. His poems have appeared in *Homeland: Writings About Homelessness* (FutureCycle Press); several annual anthologies: *Seasons of Change, The Mountain, A Bird in Hand, - Risk and Flight, Deep Waters, Home* (all published by Outrider Press); two anthologies of the Florida State Poets Association, among others. He was a Finalist two consecutive years in the William Faulkner - William Wisdom Poetry Contest. He composes all his poems vocally using voice-to-text software so, for him, sound is as essential as word-images. Paul lives with his wife, Beryl, in Broward County, FL

Sally Naylor, unrepentant rascal, remains a perennial gypsy. This wordsmith enjoys the water birds on her lake in Coral Springs, Florida, for now. Poet, counselor & educator, Sally taught & wrote curricula for gifted, peer counseling & AIDS education classes. Writing workshops, travel, yoga & skating tightropes keep her out of trouble. Her first collection, *Firebird* (PP Books), a story of regeneration, is available on Amazon, as are her memoir, *Rogue Nirvana* (Lioncrest Press) & two additional volumes: *Heresies & Sweet Basil* & *Riffs* (PP Books). She now hustles to complete a creative writing text that employs innovative strategies & recipes or "how to" models for fledgling writers.

Stephen Lewis Schaurer is old, three half-decades past 52, a balanced time to live and shout. He turned to poetry as a diversion from short stories (see the story *When The Brakes Went*, online at www.writecorner.com under 2007 fiction, nominated for a Pushcart award), and from his work and play on two novels-still-in-progress. His thematic preference is wet humor, spoken word and story-telling in poems. He recites at various readings and participates in O, Miami Poetry events. His poems also appear in the *SWEAT Collective* and in the anthology *Second Monday Muse*, by South Florida Poets.

Made in the USA
Columbia, SC
03 October 2018